The Manatee

2-99

DATE	ISSUED TO
JAN 2 0 2000	
JUN 1 4 2003	
AUG 1 8 2004	

DISCARD

DEMCO 32-209

THE MANATEE

THE MANATEE

Alvin, Virginia, and Robert Silverstein
and Laura Silverstein Nunn

THE MILLBROOK PRESS, BROOKFIELD, CONNECTICUT

Cover photo courtesy of Dr. Harvey Barnett/Peter Arnold, Inc.

Photographs courtesy of D.R. and T.L. Schrichte, Orlando, Fla.: pp. 10, 28, 30, 33, 51; Bridgeman/Art Resource, NY: p. 13; Fred Bavendam, Peter Arnold, Inc.: p. 17; Department of Library Service, American Museum of Natural History: pp. 20 (neg. no. 28269), 22 (neg. no. 313602, photo by Rice); Florida Dept. of Environmental Protection: pp. 25, 38 (both by Patrick M. Rose); National Biological Service, Sirenia Project: pp. 31 (James P. Reid), 36 (Sharon L. Tyson), 43 (James P. Reid), 46 (Lynn W. Lefebvre), 48 (James P. Reid); Animals/Animals: p. 54 (R.F. Head). Map by Joe LeMonnier

Library of Congress Cataloging-in-Publication Data
The manatee / by Alvin, Virginia, and Robert Silverstein
and Laura Silverstein Nunn
p.   cm.—(Endangered in America)
Includes bibliographical references and index.
Summary: Full of information on the habits and behavior of these gentle mammals, this book describes the methods being used to save the manatee from extinction.
ISBN 1-56294-551-3 (lib. bdg.) ISBN 0-7613-0163-1 (pbk.)
1. Sirenia—Juvenile literature.   2. Manatees—Juvenile literature.   3. Endangered species—Juvenile literature.
[1. Manatees.   2. Endangered species.]   I. Silverstein, Alvin.
II. Series: Silverstein, Alvin. Endangered in America.
QL737.S6M36 1995 599.5'5—dc20 95-1961 CIP AC

For Cathy Szeplaki

The authors would like to thank
Patrick M. Rose of the Florida
Department of Environmental
Protection, Division of Marine
Resources, for his careful reading
of the manuscript and his many
helpful suggestions.

CONTENTS

THE MANATEE

A manatee floats peacefully in the shallows.

THE GENTLE GIANT

For millions of years, manatees lived a peaceful existence in the shallow waters of rivers and springs in various parts of the world. No one bothered them. No one even knew what they were. Ancient sailors who spotted these creatures came home telling tales of "mermaids."

In 1493 the sailors on Christopher Columbus's ships became the first Europeans to observe these gentle giants in the New World. In the tropical waters off the Atlantic coast they observed a huge creature floating half-upright in the water, holding a baby to its breast with one flipperlike "arm." With its hairless head and broad, blunt face, it was not as beautiful as the mermaids of folktales and myths shown in paintings. But there was something humanlike about it. With a little imagination on the part of observers, the creature's high-pitched calls might sound like the siren songs of ancient myths.

ONLY ONE ENEMY

Manatees are harmless, slow-moving mammals with no natural enemies. They never had a need to defend themselves—until they were introduced to humans. Long before European explorers discovered the lands of the Western Hemisphere, Native Americans were hunting manatees. Ancient ceremonial pipes carved in the shape of manatees show the importance of these animals to their culture. They used manatee hides to make leather war shields, shoes, and even canoes. Most of all, they hunted manatees for their meat. One manatee could feed an entire village for several days.

After Spanish explorers and settlers established colonies in Florida and the Caribbean, they too found many important uses for manatees. As Roman Catholics, they were not allowed to eat meat on Fridays, but they could eat fish. In those days anything that swam in the sea was considered a fish—so the settlers could eat manatee meat on Fridays without breaking the rules of their religion. South American missionaries used manatee oil to burn in their lamps. The Spanish believed that the manatee's inner ear bones had magical powers. Crushed into powder and swallowed, the bones were believed to cure pains in the side. These bones were also thought to have the power to reduce the pain of childbirth, as well as the

Early sailors who saw manatees for the first time thought
the creatures were "mermaids" or "sirens," hence
the scientific classification of the manatee as *Sirenia*.

ability to conjure up rain. Even today, in parts of Central and South America, the bones are worn as good-luck charms against evil.

Manatees soon became a real "money maker." In the 1800s, museums paid as much as $100 for a manatee's skeleton and another $100 for its hide. This made the manatee one of the most valuable animals a hunter could seek. But increased hunting took a heavy toll. By the twentieth century, it became clear that the manatee was coming close to extinction.

BELATED CONCERN

As the population of manatees dwindled, people finally began to take a special interest in saving these gentle water creatures. Soon laws and regulations protecting manatees came into effect. Unfortunately, passing laws to prohibit hunting did not solve the problem. Gradually, it was realized that hunting was only one small danger to the manatees' survival. As more people moved into manatee territories, they brought new dangers such as speedboats, floodgates, and fishing gear that could tangle and trap the manatees. The mere presence of people and their buildings and roads changed the environment, providing manatees with less food and living space.

Many programs have been established in the effort to save the manatee. Marine biologists are studying the nature and habits of manatees, trying to find out what conditions they need to survive and how they can best be provided. Using radio tags and catalogs of the scar patterns of individual manatees, they have been tracking the animals' movements. Captive breeding programs have been set up, but so far such programs are not a major focus as they are in efforts to save certain other endangered species. Instead of concentrating on bringing new manatees into the world, one of the main objectives of these programs has been to help save the manatees already in the habitat, injured, and in need of assistance. The breeding facilities are used mainly for temporary care in manatee rescue and rehabilitation programs.

Perhaps the most important part of the fight to save the manatee is education. The more people know about manatees and their needs, the better chance these gentle giants have of escaping extinction.

WHAT IS A MANATEE?

Manatees are commonly known as sea cows because they graze in pastures of water grasses, much as cows graze on grasslands. The manatees that live in the coastal waters of the southern United States (especially Florida) belong to a species called the West Indian manatee. They can also be found in the warm waters of the Caribbean Islands (the "West Indies"), as well as eastern Central America and Brazil. Several rather closely related species live in other warm parts of the world. All belong to a group that scientists classify as the order Sirenia.

Four types of sirenians still roam the waters today. They include the West Indian manatee, the West African manatee, the Amazonian manatee, and the dugong. However, there was once a fifth kind of sirenian called Steller's sea cow, which became extinct in 1768.

DIFFERENT TYPES OF MANATEES

The West Indian manatee (*Trichechus manatus*) is the most commonly described manatee. One subspecies, the Florida manatee, is found primarily in the coastal waters of Florida and the Bahamas. Another subspecies,

The manatees who live in the coastal waters of the southern United States, especially Florida, belong to a species called the West Indian manatee.

the Antillean manatee, lives in the Caribbean Sea and the coastal waters of Brazil.

The manatee is one of the few sea mammals capable of swimming freely between fresh and salt waters. Its seal-shaped body, ranging from gray to brown in color, is enormous, growing up to 13 feet (4 meters) long and weighing as much as 3,500 pounds (1,600 kilograms). It has a thick, wrinkled hide, which is nearly hairless except for the stiff whiskers on its large snout. Its upper lip is divided into halves and closes down on its food like pliers.

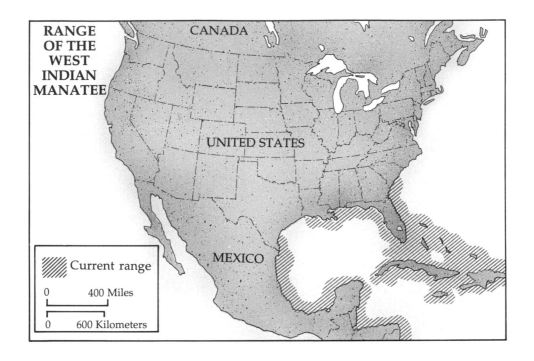

RANGE OF THE WEST INDIAN MANATEE

CANADA

UNITED STATES

MEXICO

Current range

0   400 Miles

0   600 Kilometers

The West Indian manatee is able to swim freely by moving its round, paddle-shaped tail up and down. Manatees use their powerful tails for swimming. Their front flippers are often held close to the body or used to help them steer through the water. At the end of each flipper are three or four fingernails which make the manatee unique in the underwater world. These flippers are also useful in gathering food into the manatee's mouth.

The West African manatee (*Trichechus senegalensis*), found in the coastal waters and rivers of western Africa, is similar in appearance and habits to the West Indian manatee. Not much is known about the size and location of West African manatee populations, but they seem to be declining.

The Amazonian manatee (*Trichechus inunguis*), found in the Amazon River, lives only in fresh water—unlike West Indian and West African manatees. The Amazonian's skin is smooth, and its flippers have no nails.

The dugong (*Dugong dugon*), found in the coastal waters of the Indian and Pacific oceans, is the only sirenian that lives strictly in salt water. Its skin is also smooth, and it has a notched tail similar to a dolphin. Like the Amazonian manatee, it has no nails on its flippers.

Fossils (preserved remains of ancient creatures) show that dugongs once lived in the Western Hemisphere too. But they died out millions of years ago, and only manatees remained. Scientists speculate that this may have happened because the manatees had more wear-resistant teeth and could handle freshwater vegetation better.

TOO LATE FOR THE STELLER'S SEA COW

The Steller's sea cow (*Hydrodamalis gigas*) was the only sirenian species that lived in cold water. It was also larger than all other manatees, growing

Do Steller's Sea Cows Still Exist?

SINCE the mid-1700s there have been a few sightings of animals that looked like giant manatees in the Bering Sea and off the coast of British Columbia. Perhaps some Steller's sea cows escaped mass huntings and their descendants still survive in remote parts of the Arctic.

A depiction of the Steller's sea cow, which is believed to have become extinct fewer than thirty years after its discovery.

up to 30 feet (9 meters) long and weighing up to 4 tons! The Steller's sea cow had a forked tail (so it was actually a dugong) and, unlike the other sirenians, it had no functional teeth. It fed on giant kelp, plantlike water organisms.

In 1741 the Steller's sea cow was discovered by Russians exploring the cold waters of the Bering Strait. During their journey, the Russians encountered a terrible storm and became shipwrecked. To battle the cold weather and starvation, the explorers hunted the sea cows for food. The

Only the Name Lived On

GEORG WILHELM STELLER, a German who was educated in botany and medicine, was one of the men on the shipwrecked voyage to the Bering Strait. He was the only one who became fascinated with the sea cows beyond their usefulness as food. During the time he spent on the island, Steller wrote notes about the sea cows' appearance and habits. He noted that they stayed together in groups and protected each other from danger. When Steller returned home, no one seemed very impressed with his intriguing observations. It was not until after his death that this species of sea cow was given his name.

animals actually saved the explorers' lives. When the weather finally warmed up, the sailors managed to build a small boat from the remains of their ship and sailed home. When they returned, they told others about the big sea cows. Before long, numerous hunters were killing these animals for food and profit. By 1768 there were no more sea cows to be found. The Steller's sea cow became extinct fewer than thirty years after its discovery.

EVOLUTION OF THE MANATEE

Manatees may have earned the nickname "sea cow" because of their eating habits, but their closest living relatives are actually elephants.

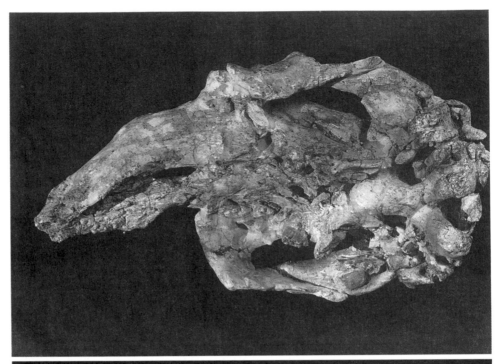

A Sirenian skull fossil discovered in Florida in 1929.

In fact, scientists believe that the ancestors of the manatees were four-footed land animals that returned to the sea about sixty million years ago. (Manatees are not fish; they are mammals, which have lungs for breathing air and feed their young with milk made in their bodies.)

Over the generations, after the manatees' ancestors returned to live in the water, their bodies gradually changed. The offspring who developed characteristics that made them better suited to life in the water survived to mate and have young of their own. The new generations remained air-breathing mammals, but their lungs grew larger and more efficient, able to exchange carbon dioxide and other bodily waste products for oxygen from the air during the brief time they surfaced to breathe. Other changes helped them adapt to life in the water. Their front legs became flippers, with only their internal bone structure and their nails to show that they had once had separate "fingers." Their back legs disappeared and a paddle-shaped tail developed, similar to the tails of whales. A layer of blubber under the skin provided insulation and helped to produce a streamlined shape, well adapted to slipping smoothly through the water.

MANATEE SENSES

Manatees have the five senses that humans have, but they use them differently. For example, they depend less on their vision than we do. Thin inner membranes can be used to cover their eyes underwater, almost like protective goggles. In very clear water, manatees can spot things at distances up to 115 feet (30 meters), and studies have shown that they can distinguish between different-sized objects and different colors and different patterns.

Although they have no external ears—just small slits on the sides of the head—their hearing is remarkably keen. They can hear noises from far distances, but unlike whales and dolphins, they do not seem to use echolocation (sending out sounds and mapping the patterns of the sound waves that bounce back off objects) to find their way. In fact, they sometimes bump into things as they swim through the muddy shallow waters. They do make sounds underwater and use them to communicate with other manatees.

Manatees have "whiskers," called vibrissae, all over their bodies. These whiskers are extremely sensitive to touch and are used as feelers in identifying food or exploring the sea bottom. Manatees close their nostrils when they go underwater, but they use a kind of combined chemical sense, smell-taste, to choose foods to eat and to identify other manatees. The manatee's smell-taste is especially useful during mating. The male uses this special sense to locate a female after she has left her special scent on underwater objects, announcing that she is ready to mate.

MANATEES AS AIR-BREATHING WATER MAMMALS

Although they spend their whole lives in the water, manatees need to breathe air to live. So they must come up to the surface to breathe. The oxygen from the air helps to release energy from food chemicals. So the more active manatees are, the more air their bodies require. (A very active manatee may have to surface to breathe every thirty seconds, while during a rest period it can hold its breath for as long as twenty minutes.) Since manatees live in shallow waters, they don't have to rise very high for air, even when they have been resting on the bottom.

Typically, manatees spend from two to twelve hours each day resting, either floating near the surface or lying on the bottom. During long rests underwater, their bodies conserve energy by slowing down; their heartbeat rate drops from its normal fifty to sixty beats per minute to only thirty beats. Surfacing for air is such an automatic action that manatees can rise for a quick breath then sink back to the bottom without really leaving their quiet, sleeplike state. They can even rise to the surface and sink to the bottom without moving their tails or flippers, by expanding or

A manatee's whiskers, or vibrissae, are used as feelers for identifying food along the sea bottom.

compressing the air in their lungs. (Manatees' lungs are rather muscular, and the diaphragm—a sheetlike muscle at the bottom of the chest—is very strong.)

Manatees' lungs exchange half of the stale air for fresh air in each breath. (Human lungs normally exchange less than 10 percent of the air in each breath.) Manatees' efficient breathing allows them to put on bursts of speed, up to 15 miles (24 kilometers) per hour when necessary; normally they cruise along at 2 to 5 miles (3 to 8 kilometers) per hour.

Marching Teeth

SINCE THE MANATEES' diet consists mainly of gritty water plants, and they chew their food thoroughly before swallowing, their teeth wear down. Fortunately, they never need a dentist because they have a nearly endless supply of teeth! When their big grinding molars begin to wear out, the old ones move toward the front, where they eventually fall out and are replaced by new ones. A manatee's teeth have no roots anchored to the jawbone, which allows for the "marching teeth" to move through its mouth just like a conveyor belt.

WHAT DO THEY EAT?

Manatees are primarily plant-eating mammals. They consume 10 to 15 percent of their body weight—as much as 100 pounds (45 kilograms) of plant food each day. They have to spend six to eight hours a day eating to satisfy their enormous appetites. Although their main diet is vegetarian, manatees sometimes swallow little crabs, snails, or other small animals that cling to the water grasses they eat. Since their grass diet has such a low nutritional value, these little "bonuses" add protein to their diet.

The manatee's metabolic rate (the rate of the chemical reactions in its body) is rather low compared with other mammals. This is an adaptation to life on a rather poor-quality diet in warm waters where there is less of a need to use food energy to produce body heat. But this adaptation carries some disadvantages. With their low metabolic rate, manatees cannot tolerate cold very well; so a sudden cold snap may kill them. And their healing of wounds, such as a gash made from a boat propeller, is slow.

A MANATEE'S LIFE

Manatees are not usually very sociable mammals. They spend their days eating, resting, and traveling the waters on their own. However, in certain situations manatees do congregate. They may come together in temporary groups of mixed sexes and ages. Young males, not quite ready to mate, may form "bachelor herds." In these loose groupings there is no real social structure—no individual takes the role of a leader, and there are no social classes in particular. But if one manatee starts doing something that looks like fun, others may follow. One small group of manatees at Blue Lagoon Lake, for example, was observed bodysurfing for more than an hour, with squeals and squeaks and nuzzling between rides. Manatees that meet may also "kiss" and mouth each other and play games of bumping and chasing. They form longer-lasting social groupings during mating, raising their young, and migrating to warmer climates.

READY FOR MATING

Female manatees may be ready to mate at the age of four or five, but usually are not able to raise young successfully until they are seven or

While manatees are not known for being very sociable animals,
when they meet they may bump or "kiss" each other.

eight years old. There is no regular mating season. However, when the female is in estrus, or ready to mate, she rubs various parts of her body that contain special scent glands onto rocks, logs, or other objects found in the water. This becomes her "message center." It announces to any passing male manatees (bulls) the readiness of the female to breed and where she can be located.

Male manatees spend much of their time roaming over long distances, checking on the various females on their route through the river system. The bulls are able to track down a female in estrus by following her chemical trail in the water. All the female has to do is wait for her suitors. As many as a dozen bulls may show up to court the female. They form a "mating herd" that may stay together for as long as a month. For most of this time the female tries to flee from the males in the herd, and some of the younger males may get impatient and leave. But the persistent older bulls are rewarded for their patience when the female is finally ready to mate. In some species, male animals fight for a mate, but that is not the case for the easygoing manatees. The bulls do not need to compete for the female because she is willing to mate with each of them in turn.

Once the bulls have mated with the female, they leave and return to their normal routine. The female will have the job of bearing and raising the young. A manatee's pregnancy lasts about thirteen months. She gives birth to one calf or, more rarely, twins. The baby nurses from its mother's two teats, which are located just under her flippers.

BONDING BETWEEN A MOTHER AND HER CALF

The relationship between the mother and her calf is very close. The calf rarely leaves its mother's side. Communication plays an important role in their lives together.

**The relationship between a manatee mother and calf
is very close for the first two years of the calf's life.
This manatee mother is shown nursing her calf.**

Touching is an essential form of communication between the mother and her calf. They constantly show affection toward one another, holding with their flippers and engaging in gentle kisses, very much like human mothers and babies. They even play together. The calf frequently rides around on its mother's back. They also play games such as tag, bodysurfing, and barrel rolling. The mother is her calf's best friend for the first two years of its life.

Vocalization is another key part of the communication between the mother and her calf. They vocalize through squeaks and squeals. There seems to be constant chatter between the two mammals, since the mother likes to keep in continuous contact with her calf. (According to one eyewitness report, a mother manatee and her calf, accidentally separated by a canal lock, called to each other continuously for three hours until the gate was opened.) Mother manatees are highly protective of their young and have been known to respond to their calf's squeal up to 200 feet (60 meters) away.

Manatee cow and calf at Crystal River, Florida.

During the first two years of the calf's life, the mother is responsible for socializing her baby, as well as for teaching it some of life's most important survival lessons—such as what to eat, where to eat, and where to migrate. Once the calf has learned all it can from its mother, it will wander away one day and begin a life on its own.

MANATEES PREPARE FOR MIGRATION

Each year, the lives of manatees are disrupted by the onset of cold weather. Since vegetation is scarcer during the winter, manatees spend a great deal of time eating during the fall, adding on hundreds of pounds of extra fat to their bodies. They have a remarkable ability to store fat, allowing them to fast for a long time.

Since a manatee has so much blubber, you might think that this extra fat would help to keep it warm, but actually the manatee's insulation is not very effective. When the water temperature falls below 68°F (20°C), manatees are forced to migrate to a warmer place. At their winter refuges, large groups of manatees come together.

MANATEE REFUGE HOT SPOTS

Many manatees have a few favorite places to which they migrate each winter. One popular site is Crystal River, located on the central west coast of Florida, where the weather is warm and food is plentiful. In 1983 this site became the first national wildlife refuge for manatees. Another refuge

In the winter months, the temperature of the water
gets colder and manatees migrate to warmer springs.

that attracts manatees is the Blue Spring Run, located in north central Florida. These sanctuaries have a year-round temperature of 72°F (22°C). Over the years, the number of manatees has increased greatly. This could be due to the regulations of the refuge, protecting the manatees from outside dangers such as motorboats, barges, and trespassers who might harass them.

Other gathering places that have become popular are not even natural hot springs, but rather the manmade variety. Hundreds of manatees congregate around power plants, located in various parts of Florida. In the process of producing power these power plants cool down their turbines by drawing in cool water and discharging the warm water into the canals. Once the warm weather returns, the manatees resume their normal, solitary lives.

MANATEES HAVE NO NATURAL ENEMIES

Manatees have always been described as peaceful sea creatures—gentle, shy, and trusting. They are completely defenseless, without any slashing teeth or claws or horns; their only response to danger is to swim away. Manatees react this way because they have no known natural enemies. Some scientists have speculated that alligators and sharks may have attacked manatees, but there has been no real proof of this. Manatees face more substantial dangers as a result of the changes that people have introduced in the manatee habitat.

ON THE BRINK OF EXTINCTION

For hundreds of years, the manatee population has been threatened by humans. As tourism continues to prosper in Florida, manatees are constantly placed in danger by unintentional or deliberate actions of people. If these gentle water mammals do not receive complete cooperation and understanding from the public, extinction of the manatee may be inevitable.

PEOPLE CAUSE DANGER FOR THE MANATEES

Sheer carelessness and ignorance are responsible for many injuries and deaths of manatees today. Discarded trash, such as plastic six-pack holders, plastic bags, fishing lines and hooks, are hazardous to manatees. They may become entangled in these items or swallow them, resulting in serious infections and sometimes death. Manatees may also get caught up in crab trap lines or other fishing gear used by commercial fishermen.

Floodgates and canal locks are used to control water levels. The tremendous pressure exerted on the water by opening and closing the

With no natural enemies, manatees are endangered by the careless actions of people living near manatee habitats. For example, manatees can become entangled in plastic six-pack holders and plastic bags.

gates and locks can pin or drown manatees. A number of them have been crushed and killed. In addition, a closing gate may separate a mother from a calf that is too young to survive on its own.

For years, hunting was responsible for the deaths of a large number of manatees. Manatee meat was considered a delicacy. Some muscular parts of a manatee's body are very similar to pork; others taste more like beef, and some are rather like fish. Hunting took such a toll on the manatee population that Florida declared the species "protected" in 1893. But poaching (illegal hunting) continued, especially during bad times such as the Depression of the 1930s and during World War II. Now strict rules and regulations are enforced, and the number of deaths due to illegal hunting of manatees has decreased considerably.

However, harassment by boats, divers, fishermen, and tourists still jeopardizes the safety of manatees. This "harassment" includes pursuing, chasing, grabbing, touching, riding, and even feeding manatees. The animals may become scared and leave their warm, desirable habitat and travel to colder, more dangerous waters. In addition, harassment may lead to the separation of a mother and her calf.

Tugboats, motorboats, and jet-powered water skis have been responsible for numerous injuries and deaths of manatees. Since manatees need to breathe air to live, they often rest in shallow waters. Unfortunately, when manatees are in the path of motorboats, it is often too late for these slow-moving mammals to get out of the way—even though they may hear the sound of a boat's motor approaching. Thus the manatee is likely to be hit by the boat, resulting in death, or—if it's lucky—less serious injuries, such as a cut on the skin caused by the boat's propellers. Most manatees in Florida have rather distinctive scars or deformities caused by accidents with boats. Studies have shown that collisions with boats and barges can account for one quarter of all manatee deaths. And with more than one million boats in Florida alone, this toll is likely to increase.

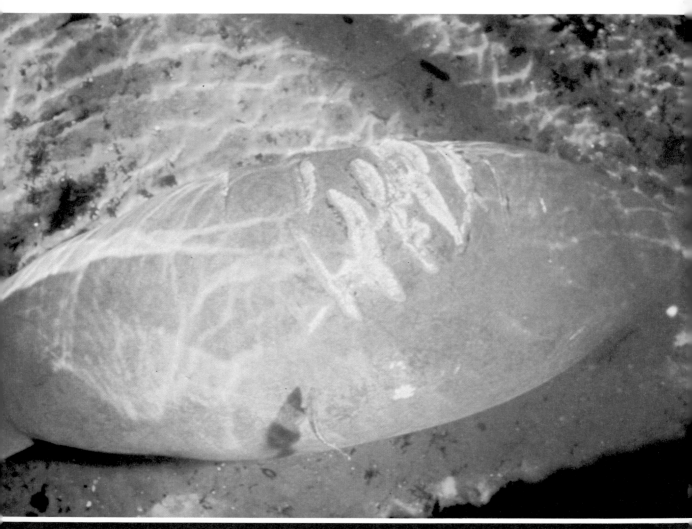

The scar pattern on this manatee's back has been caused by boat propellers. In fact, most manatees in Florida have such distinctive scar patterns caused by run-ins with boat propellers that scientists use these patterns to identify individual animals.

Nature's First Aid

WHEN A manatee's skin gets sliced up by a boat's propellers, it has a special marine adaptation that allows its blood to clot quickly. A chemical in the blood of marine animals (unlike human blood) makes it clot when water hits it. This quick-clotting blood keeps manatees from bleeding to death underwater and from attracting predators that would easily follow the scent of blood in the water.

People are not always willing to cooperate in reducing the hazards to manatees. In 1991, for example, after a manatee died from an injury caused by a jet ski in Puerto Rico, the organizers of a jet-ski tournament in St. Petersburg were required to set up a "manatee watch." The promoter considered the regulation a nuisance, complaining that people who came down to enjoy the water would be deprived of some of their fun.

MANATEES FACE NATURAL HAZARDS TOO

One natural danger that manatees have difficulty avoiding is the periodic "red tides." Algae and other microscopic organisms grow in the surface waters and are an important part of the food chain. Small marine animals feed on this surface life (called plankton), filtering it out of the water. Usually the populations of various water species stay in balance. But sometimes some of the plankton organisms, such as algae and dinoflagellates, have a sudden population explosion, multiplying in such huge numbers that they stain the water red. Marine animals such as sea squirts feed on the algae, and chemicals produced by the plankton become concentrated in the animals' bodies. But some of the chemicals produced by algae are poisonous to mammals when eaten in large amounts. And when manatees feed on water grasses, they may swallow large numbers of small marine animals along with them. In 1982 an outbreak of red tide caused the deaths of thirty-seven manatees.

Cold weather is another important factor that can threaten manatee survival. Although a manatee's body contains an enormous amount of fat, its blubber is not enough to protect it from cold temperatures. When the water temperature falls below 68°F (20°C), manatees cannot produce enough metabolic heat to make up for the heat loss. (Remember their unusually slow metabolism.) While chilling makes them more susceptible to illness, such as pneumonia, they can also die from the stress brought on by prolonged cold. Cold weather may seem like a natural, rather than a manmade hazard, but humans have had an influence here too. Manatees gather around artificial heat sources, such as the discharge from power plants. This may take them into areas where the climate is cooler, and the temperature is more likely to drop suddenly to levels they cannot tolerate.

TOO MANY PEOPLE?

Probably the most serious of all the dangers threatening the manatee's survival is the loss of habitat. As the human population continues to grow, there is an increase in water pollution, which includes litter, herbicides, pesticides, and surface runoff. They all contribute to the devastation of the manatee's feeding grounds. In addition, the construction of industrial developments has eliminated large areas of manatee habitat. Since the 1940s, 30 to 80 percent of the seagrass beds that manatees depend on have been destroyed in some areas as a result of human activities.

Manatees are at a disadvantage in trying to cope with all these dangers because of their low reproduction rate. A female does not begin producing young until she is about seven years old. Then she gives birth to only one calf every two to five years. So unless efforts are made to help them, manatees will not be able to reproduce quickly enough to make up for the numbers that are lost. In today's world, manatees can no longer exist peacefully. They need help from people just to survive.

SAVING THE MANATEE

The U.S. Fish and Wildlife Service has officially listed manatees as an endangered species, since they are dangerously close to extinction. People have also formed some private organizations to help the manatees. These groups have fought for new laws and regulations to protect manatees and their habitat. Dedicated supporters have also conducted studies and research on manatees in the effort to find more ways to help them survive.

MANATEES HAVE LOCAL PROTECTION

People became aware of the manatee's desperate need for help back in the nineteenth century. In addition to the Florida law passed in 1893 protecting manatees from harm, a 1907 regulation established a fine of $500 for anyone who killed or molested a manatee. Those laws helped to reduce the hunting problem, but gradually it was realized that more effective protection was needed.

Signs such as this one have been posted to
protect manatees in the areas where they congregate.

In 1978 the Florida state legislature passed the much stronger Florida Manatee Sanctuary Act. This act declared Florida a "refuge and sanctuary for the manatees" and stated: "It is unlawful for any person, at any time, intentionally or negligently, to annoy, molest, harass, or disturb any manatee." Recognizing the special dangers from boat collisions, the law provided for the enforcement of boat speed regulations in areas where manatees lived. Violators could be subject to fines up to $1,000 and/or sixty days in jail. The Florida Department of Natural Resources and the Florida Game and Fresh Water Fish Commission have the responsibility of enforcing these regulations.

MANATEES ARE PROTECTED AT THE FEDERAL LEVEL TOO

The federal government finally acknowledged the importance of manatee survival by passing the Marine Mammal Protection Act of 1972 and the Endangered Species Act (ESA) of 1973. The ESA makes it illegal to "harass, harm, pursue, hunt, shoot, wound, kill, capture, or collect endangered species." The law also forbids importing or exporting endangered species, their parts, or products derived from such animals. Convictions at a federal level could result in fines up to $100,000 and/or one year in prison.

Laws and regulations protecting manatees are essential to the fight against their extinction. However, manatee-saving programs, including research on the manatee's life cycle and habitat and investigations of the injuries to manatees, are vital to ensure the survival of the species.

MANATEE RESEARCH AND RECOVERY PROGRAMS

The ESA provided for the development of a Manatee Recovery Plan. This plan is coordinated by the U.S. Fish and Wildlife Service and outlines a list of tasks aimed at ending the danger to the manatee's survival. The efforts have centered on the state of Florida, which contains most of the manatee habitats within the United States.

In 1989 the governor of Florida directed the state's Department of Natural Resources to work with thirteen key counties to reduce manatee injuries and deaths. More than 80 percent of all the manatee deaths have occurred in these counties. Specific speed zones for boats were to be set up, and comprehensive local protection plans were to be developed.

The Manatee Salvage Program. The Florida Department of Natural Resources is responsible for this program, the purpose of which is to examine manatees found dead and to collect important information on them. Records are kept of the manatees' length, weight, their diet, and their cause of death. This research can lead to better ways to protect manatees from the dangers in the waters, and to set up restrictions in the places where the most manatee deaths seem to occur.

The Scar Pattern Catalog Program. This program is popular among researchers. Since most manatees have distinctive scars caused by accidents with motorboats, the scar patterns can be used to identify individual animals and trace their movements and activities. The U.S. Fish and Wildlife Service, along with the Florida Power and Light Company, Florida Audubon Society, Florida Department of Environmental Protection, and the Save-the-Manatee Club, have an identification catalog with photographs of scarred manatees that include over nine hundred individuals. The purpose of this program is to keep track of the various manatees over time to learn more about their behavior, migrations, habitat, and other aspects of their lives.

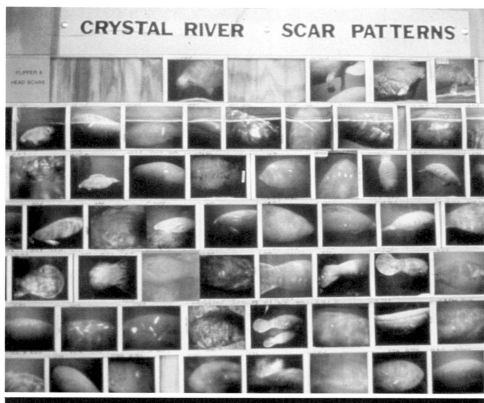

CRYSTAL RIVER - SCAR PATTERNS -

FLIPPER & HEAD SCARS

The Scar Pattern Catalog Program helps keep track of individual manatees to follow their movements and learn more about manatee behavior.

The Tagging Program. This is another research program conducted by the U.S. Fish and Wildlife Service and the Florida Department of Environmental Protection. Researchers catch manatees and carefully attach a radio tag in the form of a belt around the manatee's tail that connects to a floating transmitter. (The tag does not cause any harm or discomfort to a manatee as it swims, feeds, and rests in its daily activities.) The purpose of the tagging program is to keep track of manatees' movements, travel patterns, and habitats for up to two years. The connection is designed to avoid getting tangled, and it has a built-in weak point so that if it does get caught, the tag breaks free and no harm comes to the manatee. In addition to the distinctive radio signal of each transmitter, researchers can identify individual manatees by the special color-band combinations seen at the top of each transmitter. The problem with the tagging program is that sometimes the tag breaks off after reintroduction, and contact is lost.

———

Captive Rehabilitation and Breeding Programs. The objective of captive rehabilitation programs is to nurse sick and injured manatees back to health so that they can eventually be reintroduced into the wild. While some manatees are born in captivity, captive breeding involves a number of complications. One problem is that manatees have such a slow reproductive rate that it would be impossible to produce enough manatees to make a significant difference. Another disadvantage is that the mother needs to teach her calf very important survival skills that may be difficult to teach while in captivity. So when it is time to release the calf into the wild, the calf may not know what kinds of food to eat or where to migrate when the weather gets cold. The first captive breeding efforts were disappointing: The only two captive-born manatees released into the wild, Sunrise and Savannah, soon disappeared, and researchers fear that they did not survive.

———

Taking care of manatees in captivity also requires a lot of people, time, and money. According to estimates by the Fish and Wildlife Service in 1991, it costs about $25,000 a year to keep a healthy adult manatee in

A transmitter on a tether has been attached to the tail of this manatee.
This is another way in which scientists can monitor a manatee's movements.

A Breeding Success Story

D R. JESSE WHITE, a researcher who dedicated his life to saving the manatee, was convinced that captive breeding and the introduction of the captive-born manatees into controlled refuges held the key to the species' survival. After many failed attempts to breed manatees at the Miami Seaquarium, Dr. White discovered that diet plays an important role in successful breeding. Shortly after he added extra nutrients (calcium and phosphorus) to the diet of captive manatees, a female named Juliet became pregnant. Her calf was born in 1975, and in the following years Dr. White raised a number of captive-born and orphaned manatees.

captivity, including $10,000 for food alone. At present it seems more sensible to use available money and facilities to rescue sick and injured wild manatees rather than to keep a stock of breeding females.

So far, the captive births have been the result mainly of unplanned matings. In the future, researchers intend to conduct limited breeding studies in a more controlled, scientific manner, carefully selecting the parents to avoid inbreeding. Meanwhile, studies on releasing captive manatees are continuing. The researchers hope to achieve better survival rates by holding captive manatees longer and using "halfway houses," protected areas where captive manatees can adjust to life in the wild in a more controlled way.

FUTURE OF THE MANATEE

Learning more about manatees is vitally important for ensuring their future as a species. The more information that researchers collect, the better chance they will have of identifying the dangers, preserving the areas where manatees mainly congregate, and—most important—using the knowledge gained to educate the public about the importance of the manatees' survival and what each person can do to help.

THE PUBLIC HELPS THE MANATEE

Since there is not much that can be done about Florida's growing population, the effort to help the manatee is focusing on ways to educate the public and involve people in positive ways. Today, many schools in Florida include manatee education in their curriculum. Children are encouraged to do what they can for the manatee. A good start is to pick up the litter and trash on shores that could be swept away into the water and endanger the animals that live there.

Snooty, the first manatee born in captivity.

The Adopt-a-Manatee Program, managed by the Save the Manatee Club, is another way people can get involved. For a small fee, people can "adopt" a manatee from a list of those that winter at Blue Spring State Park in north central Florida. "Adoption" doesn't mean that people can keep a manatee as a pet, but they do receive pictures and information so they can learn all about one specific manatee. The adoption fees go directly into a fund that pays for manatee protection efforts and further research. The club also provides various educational materials, bumper stickers, and publicity about manatees.

THE SOUTH FLORIDA Museum and Bishop Planetarium is the home of Snooty, the first manatee born in captivity. In 1948, Snooty was born during an attempt to save his injured, pregnant mother. He has lived in captivity longer than any other manatee in the world. Today, people come to visit Snooty at the Bishop Museum where he plays an active part in the education of all visitors. Snooty has also participated in hearing experiments conducted by the Mote Marine Laboratory in Sarasota that have contributed to our knowledge of manatees.

OBSERVATIONS AND EXPERIMENTS ON MANATEE BEHAVIOR

Many organizations have contributed substantial efforts in the rescue and research of manatees. Sea World in Florida established a Manatee Rescue and Rehabilitation Program in 1976, becoming one of the state's leading facilities in rescue and rehabilitation. Today there is an entire statewide rescue network, including manatee hospitals equipped to diagnose and treat sick and injured manatees, with rehabilitation tanks for holding them until they have recovered enough to be returned to the wild.

In 1991, Tampa's Lowry Park Zoo opened a multimillion-dollar Manatee and Aquatic Center. There live animal exhibits are combined with a fully equipped critical care hospital and research facility. Visitors can view the manatees through glass windows that give a view of life above and below the water surface. The manatees on display share their pool with other animals found in their natural habitat, such as hooded mergansers, ruddy ducks, and other water birds. A tour of the research facility, with educational graphics and a taped narration, provides visitors with more information about manatees and the efforts to help them.

HEARING EXPERIMENTS

Dr. Edmund Gerstein at the Lowry Park Zoo has also conducted extensive research on the hearing of manatees. A manatee named Stormy participated in various hearing experiments. One experiment required Stormy to respond to hand signals directing him to swim through a wire hoop, reaching a paddle at the right of a light. Eventually he learned to respond to a tone sounded in the water. When the light turns on, Stormy indicates if he heard it by swimming to the left of the paddle, and to the right of the paddle if he didn't.

MANATEE INTELLIGENCE AND PLAY

Other organizations have conducted studies illustrating interesting behavior and habits of manatees. Dr. Dale Woodyard of the University of Windsor, Ontario, found that manatees are more intelligent than most people think. He observed that manatees are capable of recognizing various shapes, colors, and sizes. They can even remember them for up to a year.

The Lowry Park Zoo in Tampa has combined live manatee exhibits with a critical-care manatee hospital and manatee research facility.

Another observation showing the complexity of manatee behavior was made by biologist John E. Reynolds III. The manatees that he studied liked to play, particularly in an activity called "bodysurfing." They would continually ride the current downstream and then swim back up. Variations on the game included riding sideways to the current or moving diagonally across it.

Thus, researchers continue to find that manatees are not just enormous, simple "sea cows." There is still much to learn about them. Research has already played an important role in informing the public of manatees' needs. And people who have learned to know and love manatees are the best hope for the survival of these gentle sea mammals, now and in the future.

FINGERTIP FACTS

Length	Can grow up to 13 feet (4 meters) long
Weight	Weighs up to 3,500 pounds (1,600 kilograms); average adult weighs between 1,000 and 2,000 pounds (450 and 900 kilograms)
Color	Ranges from gray to brown
Food	Primarily a plant-eating mammal; sometimes eats little crabs, snails, and other small animals that cling to the water grasses
Reproduction	There is no set mating season. Females are ready to breed successfully at about 7 years of age; males are sexually mature at 3 to 4 years of age. Females produce one calf after 13 months of pregnancy; twins are rare
Care for young	The female takes full responsibility for her calf; she nurses and guides it for the first 2 years of its life. The male has no responsibility in raising the young
Range	They are found mostly in Florida; also around the Caribbean Islands, eastern Central America, and northern Brazil

Population size	An estimated 1,850 manatees in Florida
Social behavior	Mostly solitary animals, but come together in groups during mating season and migration; mothers also share strong bonds with their calves
Life span	Can live up to 60 years

FURTHER READING

Books

Clark, Margaret Goff. *The Vanishing Manatee*. New York: Dutton, 1990.

Dietz, Tim. *Call of the Siren*. Golden, CO.: Fulcrum, 1992.

O'Keefe, M. Timothy. *Manatees: Our Vanishing Mermaid*. Lakeland, FL: Larsen's Outdoor Publishing, 1993.

Sibbald, Jean H. *The Manatee*. Minneapolis: Dillon Press, 1990.

Reynolds III, John E., and Daniel K. Odell. *Manatees and Dugongs*. New York: Facts on File, 1991.

Pamphlets

"Manatee Facts," Save the Manatee Club.

"Manatees: An Educator's Guide," 4th Edition, by Nancy Sandusky, Judith Vallee, and Patti Thompson, Save the Manatee Club, 1994.

"The West Indian Manatee in Florida," by Victoria Brook Van Meter, Florida Power and Light Company, 1989.

"West Indian (Florida) Manatee," The Florida Manatee Research & Educational Foundation.

Articles

Bankson, Ross, "Gentle Giants in Trouble," *National Geographic World*, March 1992, pp. 15–16.

Brown, David O., "Siren Song," *Calypso Log*, April 1991, pp. 14–15.

Chu, Dan, "Florida's Sea Doc," *People*, July 9, 1990, pp. 74–75.

DiPerna, Paula, "A Question of Freedom," *Calypso Log*, September 1994, pp. 16–17.

"Manatee Moms," *Dolphin Log*, July 1989, pp. 8–9.

McAuliffe, Kathleen, "Saving Manatees: Researchers Take to the Air to Preserve a Threatened Species," *Omni*, October 1993, p. 18.

McClintock, Jack, "Too Nice to Live," *Life*, November 1990, pp. 42–48.

"Rumble in Manateeville," *People*, May 18, 1992, p. 89.

Wiley, John P., Jr., "Have You Hugged a Manatee Today?" *Smithsonian*, September 1987, pp. 92–97.

ORGANIZATIONS

The Cousteau Society
870 Greenbrier Circle, Suite 402
Chesapeake, VA 23320-2641
(804) 523-9335

Florida Department of Environmental Protection
Division of Marine Resources
3900 Commonwealth Blvd.
Tallahassee, FL 32399-3000
(904) 922-4330

Florida Department of Environmental Protection
Blue Spring State Park
2100 West French Ave.
Orange City, FL 32763
(904) 775-3663

Florida Manatee Research & Educational Foundation
12025 North Elkcam Blvd.
Dunnellon, FL 34433
(904) 489-8142

Florida Power and Light Company
P.O. Box 029100
Miami, FL 33102-9100

Save the Manatee Club
500 North Maitland Ave., Suite 210
Maitland, FL 32751
(800) 432-JOIN

Manatee Hospitals

Homosassa Springs State Wildlife Park
9225 West Fishbowl Drive
Homosassa, FL 32646
(904) 628-2311

Lowry Park Zoological Garden
7530 North Blvd.
Tampa, FL 33604
(813) 935-8552

Miami Seaquarium
4400 Rickenbacker Causeway
Miami, FL 33149
(305) 351-5705

Sea World of Florida
7007 Sea World Drive
Orlando, FL 32821
(407) 363-2355

Manatee Hotline

If you see a manatee with a transmitter or a sick
or injured manatee, call: (800) DIAL-FMP

INDEX

ABOUT THE AUTHORS

Dr. Alvin Silverstein is a Professor of Biology at the College of Staten Island of the City University of New York.

Virginia B. Silverstein is a translator of Russian scientific literature.

The Silversteins' collaboration began with a biochemical research project at the University of Pennsylvania and since then has produced six children and more than one hundred published books that have received high acclaim from reviewers for their clear, timely, and authoritative coverage of science and health topics.

Robert Silverstein, a graduate of Rutgers University with a major in Communications, joined his parents' writing team in 1988 and has already coauthored more than two dozen books with them. He lives with his wife, Linda, and their young children, Emily and Jamey, in a small New Jersey town known for its creative artists and writers.

Laura Silverstein Nunn, a graduate of Kean College with a major in Sociology, has been helping with the research for her parents' books since her high school days and has recently joined the Silverstein writing team. She lives with her husband, Matt, and their baby son, Cory, in a rural New Jersey town not far from her childhood home.